To my dear friend, the
horticulturalist?. With love
& admiration, Yvonne. Aug, 2001

THE MASTERS' BOOK OF BONSAI

THE MASTERS' BOOK OF Bonsai

by
DIRECTORS OF THE JAPAN BONSAI ASSOCIATION

Nobukichi Koide

Saburō Katō

Fusazō Takeyama

KODANSHA INTERNATIONAL
Tokyo • New York • London

Distributed in the United States by Kodansha America, Inc., 114
Fifth Avenue, New York, N.Y. 10011, and in the United Kingdom
and continental Europe by Kodansha Europe Ltd., 95 Aldwych,
London WC2B 4JF. Published by Kodansha International Ltd.,
17-14, Otowa 1-chome, Bunkyo-ku, Tokyo 112, and Kodansha
America, Inc. Copyright © 1967 by Kodansha International Ltd.
All rights reserved. Printed in Japan.

LCC 67-12585
ISBN 0-87011-453-0
ISBN 4-7700-0922-4 (in Japan)

First edition, 1967
First paperback edition, 1983
  96 97 98 99 15 14

TABLE OF CONTENTS

ACKNOWLEDGEMENTS

THE authors of this book express their sincere gratitude to the members of the Bonsai Association and also to the bonsai growers who have kindly granted permission to photograph the treasures of their art.

Thanks are also due to Mr. Takashi Inoue for his time and effort in effecting liaison between the authors and the publisher, and also to Mr. Yoshiaki Jinguji, whose excellent photography has enhanced the value of this book.

INTRODUCTION

What is Bonsai?

Bonsai is a tree or plant cultured in a container and is therefore small in size, but yet in its entirety expresses the beauty and volume of a tree grown in a natural environment. The literal meaning of bonsai is "planted in a tray."

The difference between bonsai and ordinary potted plants is that the latter are usually plant species in which the flowers or leaves are the focus of appreciation, while with the former, the beauty of the entire tree and its harmony with the container in which it is planted is the matter of esthetic concern.

The bonsai may be only a foot tall, but still may have the exact features of a towering tree found high in the mountains, or a form similar to the lonely windswept pine that clings to a cliff above an isolated seashore. There are various styles of bonsai, but, like trees found in their natural environment, no two are exactly identical. Bonsai with straight thick trunks, slanting trunks, double or triple trunks, etc.—all of these forms are seen in nature. Bonsai, in other words, is an attempt to artificially perfect natural tree forms in miniature. A recent trend in bonsai is to create even the feeling of a forest by group-planting a number of trees in a tray, and to plant trees and shrubs on an interestingly shaped rock to produce the impression of plant life on a rocky terrain.

The History of Bonsai

The first mention of bonsai appears in Kamakura period (1192–1333) records of the Kasuga Shrine. An illustration of bonsai is seen in the famous picture scroll of the priest Hōnen of the same period. The illustration shows trees in their natural form planted in basins and displayed on a shelf. This clearly indicates that bonsai were being cultured for the purpose of appreciation at this time. The picture scroll was produced during the Kamakura period, but it mainly illustrates life in the Heian period (794–1191), which means that bonsai probably existed even that long ago.

Various essays written since the Kamakura period mention that trees and plants were gathered from the fields and mountains and made into bonsai. A famous Nō play entitled Hachi-no-ki *(plants in a pot), which deals with subjects of the same period, refers to plum, cherry, and pine as the trees planted in a pot. This also is evidence that the appreciation of bonsai dates back some eight hundred years.*

It is noted that during the Edo period (1615–1867), gardening and potted plants, especially flowering plants and species with colored leaves, were extremely popular and were developed greatly. The interest in bonsai, however, was apparently limited and showed very little progress. However, with the heightening interest in Southern Sung-style painting and the popularity of literati art at the end of the Edo period, bonsai also was frequently used as the subject matter for painting and poetry. On the other hand, however, oddly deformed trees were mistakenly considered as good bonsai, and the collection of these species became a fad for a short period. This tendency was soon corrected, and bonsai based on the expression of healthy, natural beauty was revived.

To cope with the growing interest in bonsai by the general public, the first nationwide bonsai exhibition was held in Tokyo in 1914. And in 1934, an annual exhibition emphasizing creative bonsai was initiated at the Tokyo Metropolitan Art Museum and is being continued even today.

Bonsai was once considered a leisurely hobby for the rich only. Now, however, it is accepted by the general public as an art, as well as a hobby, and has become particularly popular with people living in the crowded city areas, who otherwise have few direct contacts with nature. Interest is also growing in the United States and other foreign countries, and requests from enthusiasts outside Japan for tools, equipment and technical advice have greatly increased.

The Art of Bonsai

Bonsai is essentially the art of choosing a plant which has the potential of becoming a good bonsai, then growing it under complete, constant, and affectionate care so that it blends with the container in which it is planted to express a natural beauty. It follows, then, that adequate sunshine, water, fertilizer, and suitable soil are necessary for healthy growth. At the same time, careful trimming, pruning, repotting, wir-

ing, and other techniques are required to form the trees into the desired shape. As the result of such care, miniature growth is finally accomplished. Miniaturizing, however, is not the aim of growing bonsai, but the consolidated result of efforts to grow a healthy tree, providing correct and timely training for the specimen. The tree should be made small, but adequate nourishment should always be provided; thus the tree is not deprived for the purpose of dwarfing. If existing bonsai were not healthy and strong, how could they have lived for hundreds of years?

Bonsai, as explained in later chapters, are variously grown from seed, collected from nature, grafted, and layered and divided. The ultimate goal is to cultivate plants by the above methods so that they are small in size, yet have the appearance of being seasoned and aged. The special characteristic of bonsai is that they express the various features of natural trees, even though cultured in an artificial environment.

How is miniaturizing possible? A single technique is not adequate to make a tree small. The fact that the plant is grown in a container, and also the trimming, pruning, repotting, trunk correction, and other care given the tree—all contribute to the final result of healthy, but limited, growth. Dwarfed trees are often found even in a natural environment. In bonsai, this environment is provided artificially and purposely, but with a good knowledge of the botanical principles of growth.

Following are some of the main factors which contribute to the limited growth of bonsai plants.

Soil and the Root

Bonsai are grown in a bowl or basin, the size of which determines the amount of soil the roots are able to grow in. This environment definitely restricts growth. The growth of the roots and accordingly its functions are restricted to the size of the container. Therefore, the nourishment and water the roots are able to absorb and transport to the tree are controlled, thus limiting growth. Plants by nature grow in a proportionate measure above and below the ground. Therefore, a balance between roots and trunk, branches and leaves should always be maintained. If straight roots are cut, the upward growth of branches, which are the counterparts of the underground roots, is controlled and restricted. When the roots are cut, the inevitable result is less nutrition transmitted to above-ground growth. Excess nourishment to the branches and leaves is passed on to the roots and helps growth underground. In other words, cutting the roots sets up a cycle by which growth of the entire tree is restricted. A good balance between growth above and below the ground must therefore always be considered. This means that the container for a bonsai must be carefully selected in terms of depth and size. Repotting also plays an important role, as fresh soil can be provided and excess roots can be cut at this time.

Trimming and Pruning

The main object of trimming and pruning, of course, is to shape the bonsai into a desired form. However, these measures also serve the purpose of reducing growth above ground in order to maintain a balance with root growth. When growing branches are trimmed, this immediately reflects upon the development of the roots and initiates a cycle similar to that set up when the roots are cut.

Sunshine

Strong sunshine, especially the ultra-violet ray, affects the growth of trees. This is evident in alpine plants, which do not grow tall. Therefore, except in special cases, such as immediately after repotting, extensive trimming, etc., bonsai should be placed on elevated shelves and exposed to sunshine throughout the day. Daily exposure to direct sunshine does restrict growth to a certain extent. Placing bonsai on an elevated shelf also provides an ideal condition for viewing the plant. Sunshine, of course, is a natural necessity for plant growth, but it is an interesting coincidence that it also serves to control excessive growth in bonsai.

Watering

When bonsai are exposed to sunshine, the soil dries fast. If constant watering is provided, as in the case of some trees found in their natural state, bonsai will grow tall. Therefore, watering should be controlled. Plants, of course, cannot survive without water, and bonsai requires daily watering, but the amount should be controlled.

Ventilation

Strong winds also play a decisive role in restricting plant growth. Note that trees high up in the mountains or growth near the windy seashore do not grow very tall. Bonsai placed on elevated shelves are exposed to the same condition, although of course in a much milder degree. Good ventilation causes the soil in which the bonsai is planted to dry faster, and therefore also serves as an indirect element in limiting plant growth.

BONSAI MASTERPIECES

Black Pine (Formal
upright style)
Height: 28″
Container: Red un-
　glazed earthenware;
　19″ × 13″ × 4″

19

◀Red Plum
Height: 26″
Container: Basin with
  overglaze enamel
  ration

Wild Plum▶
Height: 27″
Container: Red un-
  glazed earthenware
  basin

21

◄*Ezo* Spruce (Rock-grown style)
Height: 24″
Container: Oval bronze tray; 24″ (diameter)

Five-needle Pine (Cascading style)▶
Height: 28″
Container: Unglazed "raven clay" bowl

◄*Momiji* Maple
Height: 32″
Container: Oval *kinyo*-glazed
  basin; 22″ (diameter)

Dwarf Azalea►
Height: 21″
Container: Blue *(ruri)*
  glazed basin; 16″×9″×5″

25

◀Zelkova Tree (Broom style)
Height: 25″
Container: Bowl with green and blue vari-colored glaze; 20″×9″

Beech (Group planting style)▶
Height: 31″
Container: *Tokoname* ware basin; 24″×18″

26

27

28

◀Five-needle Pine
Height: 23″
Container: Unglazed "raven
 clay" pot; 17″×11″×6″

Sargent Juniper▶
Height: 32″
Container: Unglazed (Chinese)
 earthenware basin;
 18″×12″×6″

◀Winter Jasmine
Height: 24″
Container: Green-glazed
  pot

Miniatures▶
top, left: Dandelion; right:
Japanese carpinus
center, left: Reeves spiraea;
right: Lilac
bottom, left to right; *Momiji*
maple, violet, and Platan-
thera
Shelf: 14″ × 17″

◀Hemlock Spruce and Grasses
Height (hemlock spruce): 28″
Container: Reddish-purple
  unglazed earthenware basin;
  19″×11″×4″

Pourthiaea▶
Height: 23″
Container: Bowl with
  excised design; 17″×9″×7″

33

Ezo Spruce▶
Height: 41″
Container: Deep-green unglazed earthenware
        basin; 26″ × 14″ × 3″

Marsh Marigold
Height: 9″
Container: *Nameko*-glazed basin; 23″ × 14″ × 20″

36

◄Five-needle Pine
Height: 30″
Container: Lightly glazed basin
    29″ × 17″ × 5½″

Five-needle Pine (Literati style)
Height: 31″
Container: Bowl with Carved and decorated areas

37

◀Five-needle Pine (Twin trunk)
Height: 26″
Container: Deep-purple burnished pot; 17″ × 12″ × 6″

Needle Juniper (Triple trunk)▶
Height: 21″
Container: Square Shigaraki ware basin; 21″ × 14″ × 5″

39

◀*Kaede* Maple
Height: 26″
Container: White cochin ware; 20″×14″×4″

Ivy
Height: 25″
Container; Blue-glazed square pot; 12″×12″
  ×7″

41

Japanese Judas Tree
Height: 14″
Container: Yellow Cochin ware; 16″ × 8″ × 2″

BONSAI STYLES

BONSAI STYLES

Bonsai are classified by growth patterns into various styles. Some styles may seem strange and unnatural, but all are based on growth patterns found in the natural environments. The natural form and the species of the tree must be considered, therefore, to train a bonsai to form any specific style. Following are examples of some of the representative styles.

Formal Upright *(chokkan)*   Five-needle Pine
  Height: 30″
  Container: 19″ × 12¾″ × 4″, red unglazed earthen-
    ware
  Ideally, a *chokkan* bonsai has a single, upright
trunk that tapers toward the top. The branches
should be symmetrically balanced and well spaced.

Informal Upright *(moyōgi)*   Corticate Pine
  Height: 29¾″
  Container: 21½″ × 17¾″ × 4″, lightly glazed earth-
    enware
  The *moyōgi* bonsai has a single trunk with well-
balanced and wholesome curves, which should be
less pronounced toward the top of the tree.

Twin Trunk *(sōkan)* Five-needle Pine
  Height: 22½″
  Container: 14″ × 10″ × 4″, red unglazed earthen-
    ware

The *sōkan* bonsai has two trunks growing from a single root, with one trunk called the "parent" and the other the "child." Whether such a tree is a good bonsai or not depends upon the esthetic balance of the trunk thicknesses. Trees with three and five trunks are called *sankan* and *gokan* respectively.

Slanting *(shakan)* Five-needle Pine
  Height: 21¾″
  Container: 13½″ diameter, brown-glazed earthen-
    ware

The *shakan* bonsai is cultivated at a slant, with either a thick or thin trunk. It differs from the wind-swept *(fukinagashi)* style in that branches grow on both sides of the tree.

STYLES   47

Multiple Trunk *(kabudachi)*   Five-needle Pine
   Height: 18½″
   Container: 14″×9¼″×3½″, red unglazed earthenware
   The *kabudachi* bonsai has multiple trunks growing from a single root. A bonsai with multiple trunks, which includes the double, triple, and quintuple types described above, are called *kabudachi.*

Sinuous *(netsuranari)*   Five-needle Pine
   Height: 16⅝″
   Container: 20½″ diameter
   The *netsuranari* bonsai has numerous trees growing from a single serpentine root. Five-needle pines are most commonly used.

Exposed Root *(neagari)*   Sargent Juniper
   Height: 24½″
   Container: 10⅝″ diameter, unglazed earthen-
      ware footed bowl
   The *neagari* bonsai has roots growing out
of the ground, giving the trunk an unusual ap-
pearance.

Raft *(ikada)*   Five-needle Pine
   Height: 30½″
   Container: 29″ × 17½″ × 5⅜″, lightly glazed
      earthenware
   The *ikada* bonsai is made by burying the
trunk horizontally and arranging the branches
so they will appear as trunks. It is possible to
make new roots grow from the old trunk and
branches if sufficient fertilizer and care are
given to the trees. In effect, this type is similar
to the *netsuranari*.

STYLES   49

Windswept *(fuki-nagashi)* Five-needle Pine

   Height: $17\frac{1}{2}''$
   Container: $13\frac{1}{8}''$ $\times 9\frac{3}{4}'' \times 4''$, burnished red earthenware

   The *fukinagashi* bonsai has all its branches "swept" in one direction, as though it were being continually blown by strong winds.

Literati *(bunjingi)* Five-needle Pine
   Height: $37\frac{3}{4}''$
   Container: $22\frac{1}{2}''$ diameter, shallow earthenware bowl

The *bunjingi* bonsai has an upright trunk bare of branches except at the top. It is characterized by a tasteful, simple elegance.

Cascade *(kengai)* Five-needle Pine
   Height: $46\frac{3}{4}''$
   Container: $16\frac{5}{8}''$ diameter, burnished red earthenware

The *kengai* bonsai is characterized by arching or "cascading" trunk and branches. It is usually placed in a deep pot to give a sense of balance to its unusual form.

Broom *(hōkidachi)* Zelkova

The *hōkidachi* bonsai has an upright trunk with its branches trained into a fan-like shape. It resembles a broom standing on its handle.

Group *(yose-ue)* Beeches

Height: 22¼″

Container: 22½″ diameter, shallow oval blue-glazed earthenware basin

The *yose-ue* bonsai is a group of trees planted in a shallow tray to represent roadside trees, a grove, or a forest. Usually, trees of related species are used, but occasionally evergreen and deciduous trees are mixed for effect.

STYLES   51

Rock-Grown *(ishitsuki)*   Maple
  Height: 20¼″
  Container: 21¾″ diameter, oval glazed earthen-
    ware
  There are two types of *ishitsuki*. This example
shows the root of the maple firmly grasping a rock
and extending into the soil.

Rock-Grown *(ishitsuki)*   Ezo Spruce
  Height: 19¾″
  Container: 23¾″ major axis, oval brass basin
  This type of *ishitsuki* have become extremely
popular in recent years. Shrubs of Ezo spruce, in this
example, are planted in composition with the shape
of the rock to resemble growth on a rocky terrain.

BONSAI GROWING TECHNIQUES

Chapter 1

GROWING BONSAI FROM SEED *(mishō)*

T HE method of growing bonsai from seed is known as *mishō*. Once the species of tree you plan to grow has been selected, you plant the seed, watch it sprout, and train the plant with care into the type of bonsai desired. This method requires time and patience, but it is also more satisfying.

In one sense, all plants growing naturally in the mountains and fields are *mishō*, and "natural" plants collected for bonsai (*yamadori* method) could be considered *mishō* types. Ordinarily, however, this method refers to the artificial planting of seed in specially prepared ground and the control of plant growth through its various stages.

Types of Mishō
With a few exceptions, it is possible to grow almost any species of plant from its seed. Some of the more popular species in Japan are such evergreen trees as the Ezo spruce, the Japanese white (five-needle) pine, the Japanese black pine, and the Japanese red pine, and such deciduous trees as the Zelkova, the white beech, carpinus, the Sumac, and the maple.

Mishō Bonsai—Characteristics and Cultivation
Since *mishō* bonsai are grown from seed, the growing plants will exhibit the inherent characteristics of the plants from which the seed was derived. There will be some variation, therefore, in the quality of bonsai grown from seed, depending upon the seed quality.

In Japan, the proper time for planting your seed is between the middle of March and early July, the end of the rainy season. In other areas, probably early spring is the best time for planting. From two to three months are generally required for evergreen seed to sprout, and from one to two months are required for deciduous seed, after planting. These sprouts are usually kept in the same seed bed for two or three years. Once the young plants become strong enough, the better ones are selected and individually repotted.

In the seed method, your bonsai will start taking shape in about five years. With careful pruning over the years, you will be able to create magnificent bonsai from these young plants.

Planting Procedures

Let us take the five-needle pine as our example in describing *mishō* planting procedures. Whatever the species, however, the seeds should be soaked in water overnight before planting. By placing the seeds in a bowl of water you can determine which are fertile, for the fertile seeds will sink to the bottom while the "dead" seeds will float. You can be almost certain that any seeds which have tested fertile in this way will sprout and grow. Five-needle pine seeds will sprout between two and three months from the time of planting.

Seed Bed Preparation and Planting

1. To prepare the seed bed, select either a pot or wooden box, about six inches deep, that has a hole in the bottom for drainage. The drainage hole should be covered, usually with vinyl mesh, in order to improve drainage and to prevent loss of soil.

2. Secure the vinyl mesh in place with a heavy-gauge wire, bending and affixing the wire as shown in the figure.

3. Cover the bottom of the pot—about $\frac{1}{4}$ of the pot's depth—with

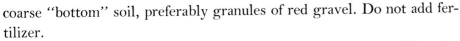

coarse "bottom" soil, preferably granules of red gravel. Do not add fertilizer.

4. Cover the bottom layer with sieved soil of the same type, filling the pot to about $\frac{1}{2}$" from the top. Again, fertilizer should not be added.

5. Place the seeds on this soil layer, roughly $1\frac{1}{2}$" apart, and cover them with fine soil to a depth of about $\frac{1}{2}$" or slightly less.

6. Water the soil well, being careful not to wash any of the topsoil from the pot.

Pot Placement and Seed Bed Care

The seed bed pot should be placed on flat ground in a sunny location protected from the wind. The seed bed should be watered regularly and weeded when necessary. When the seedlings appear, care should be taken to protect them from bugs, using sprays. A small amount of liquid fertilizer or oil-meal cake should be added to the seed bed when the seedlings are about three months old. Linseed meal, rape meal or castor meal may be tried instead. This will produce better results.

GROWING FROM SEED 57

Cultivation of Seed (Five-needle Pine)

1. By the end of one year, a five-needle pine seedling should attain a height of 2″ to 2½″, as shown. By the end of the second year, it will be only slightly taller, but will have more leaves and a thicker stem.

2. Pine seedlings should be kept in the seed bed for about two years, then repotted individually. Note the changes undergone by a bonsai through the fourth, sixth, eighth, and tenth years.

Several Bonsai Grown from Seed
From right to left above are shown a Zelkova and a wax tree, both two-year-old, three-year-old carpinus, a *kaede* maple, a Japanese black pine, and a *momiji* maple.

Chapter 2

COLLECTING PLANTS FROM
NATURE FOR BONSAI *(yamadori)*

COLLECTING trees in the mountains is called *yamadori*; making these trees into bonsai is called *yamadori-shitate*. Growing bonsai of this type will give you much pleasure as well as serve as a constant reminder of your mountain trips. Also, less time is required to achieve the end result with this method than with other methods. Another advantage of the *yamadori* method derives from actually having viewed the parent trees, which gives you a better idea of how to shape your miniature versions of them.

Collecting Season
Spring, or early summer for the high mountains, is the best season for gathering trees for bonsai. This is the time when budding starts and the trees are vigorous. For this reason, even a tree with a small root planted at this time will grow if it is given proper care.

Procedures for Digging Plants
Always be careful to dig out trees with their roots intact. Never attempt to pull them directly out of the ground. The correct procedure is to dig out the ground around the roots in such a way as to leave most of the roots intact and covered with the soil in which the tree has been growing.

Once the tree has been dug out of the ground, the branches should be

trimmed in proportion to the volume of the roots. Care in trimming should be taken so as not to spoil the overall shape of the intended bonsai. As a rule of thumb, if there are many roots, it is not necessary to trim off too many branches or leaves. But if they are few, it is necessary to trim the branches to roughly match the mass of the roots. Generally, the proportion of branches to roots is about six to four.

To keep the roots from drying out, they should be covered with sphagnum moss or moist grass. The roots of the tree with their moist covering material should be wrapped securely in strong, heavy paper or vinyl for the trip home.

Potting

To describe the correct procedure for potting, we shall take an Ezo spruce for our example. A young tree newly dug out and prepared for transport, as shown above, is called *araki*. Examples of *araki*, above left, with Ezo spruce about twenty years old seen on the left and five-needle pine

about fifteen years old seen on the right. Any trees you dig out yourself should have their roots wrapped in the same manner as shown.

1. Prepare an appropriate sized pot—an unglazed pot that will dry out easily is preferred—by covering the drainage hole with mesh and covering the bottom with coarse, lumpy soil. The size of the pot varies in accordance with the condition of the roots, the branches and the height of the tree. In this case, the diameter of the pot is 12″, while the height of the tree is 36″, a rough standard ratio for a tall tree. The pot should be filled about $\frac{1}{4}$ full with this soil. Next, a small amount of topsoil is added.

2. Unwrap your "new" tree and remove the sphagnum moss from the roots, being careful not to brush off any of the soil adhering to the roots. Trim only those roots which have been severely injured.

3. Place the tree in the pot and gradually add more topsoil. When about half full, tap the sides of the pot so that the soil will fill in open areas around the roots.

4. Fill the pot with enough soil to cover the roots, but not so full that

COLLECTING FROM NATURE   63

the topsoil will be higher than the edge. If the soil is higher than the edge, it will be washed away when you water the tree.

5. Press the soil down lightly with your fingers. Do not attempt to poke the soil down around the roots with a stick, for you may injure the small roots. Be careful not to pack the soil down too hard.

6. Spread a thin layer of sphagnum moss on the surface of the soil to prevent it and the roots from drying out.

7. After the tree is planted, it should be secured to the pot with strings so it will not shift, for newly planted trees do not have sufficient roots to hold them in place. This artificial securing of trees is called *tsuri-o-toru* or "balancing." Once the tree is secured firmly in place it will stand up well against the wind and take root more easily. These strings are even more necessary for the taller trees. Since the roots will take firm hold in about six months, the strings should be left on at least that long.

8. Finally, both the soil and the tree are watered. The soil should be watered first, then the entire tree from the top down. Reversing this procedure may result in the tree's falling over, so care should be taken to do it properly.

Post-potting Care
Newly potted trees should be placed either in a partially shaded place or under a march-reed screen where direct sunshine or strong winds will not affect them. Because the soil in the pots will not dry out easily until the trees firmly take root, watering should be done only about twice a day. Do not wet the soil too much. This stage is one of waiting for new roots to appear.

Chapter 3

GROWING CUTTINGS *(sashiki)*

T HE cultivation of cuttings for bonsai is known as *sashiki*. This method requires less time than that for growing bonsai from seeds. It also allows you to better visualize the final result.

Types of Cuttings
Cuttings for bonsai may be taken from almost any kind of suitable tree. Some of the more hardy, interesting species are listed below.

Evergreen: Ezo spruce, needle juniper, cryptomeria, Sargent juniper, Japanese cypress, cape gardenia, dwarf kumquat, Pyracantha, rock cotoneaster, and dwarf azalea

Deciduous: winter jasmine, *momiji* maple, Japanese bush clover, Japanese azalea, dogwood, flowering quince, lilac, Potentilla fruticosa, Thunberg berberry, pomegranate, mulberry, and crapemyrtle

Selecting Cuttings
Cuttings are usually taken from grown bonsai, but they can, of course, also be taken from ordinary trees. It is important to select the small branches to be used as cuttings for their vigor and leafiness. Cuttings of this kind will take root more quickly and grow faster. If the cuttings are to be taken from a deciduous tree when it is bare of leaves, select either the top of a small tree or the tips of strong branches. Above all, make sure you consider the final form of the bonsai desired before selecting cuttings.

67

Cuttings Season

Cuttings are best taken and planted either in early spring before new buds appear or, in Japan, during the June rainy season when the trees have leafed. Some species of flowering quince are best planted in mid-September. A few species are so strong and vigorous that cuttings from them can be planted almost any time of year.

Preparation and Planting of Cuttings

For our example, let us take the dogwood, a deciduous tree with pretty flowers and leaves. The flowers comprise yellow florets that hang down from stems and usually bloom in April. They are noted for their long life. The leaves are glossy on top and silver on the underside. Dogwood cuttings are very good for bonsai because of their hardiness. Although the natural tree sometimes grows to a height of thirty feet or so, the dogwood bonsai is popularly cultivated only to a height of about two feet or less.

Pot Preparation

A flower pot, or a box with drainage perforations, of suitable depth (about 5–6″) should be selected. An unglazed, porous pot is the best because it permits easier control of moisture and temperature.

1. Use red loam of a type coarser than that for *mishō* seed beds for your soil. It should be free of bacteria and fertilizer. Sift the soil to separate the coarse from the fine particles.

2. Pick small lumps from the coarse soil and fill the pot about $\frac{1}{3}$ full.

3. Fill the pot to the top with the remaining soil. The cuttings thrust into the soil will prevent the topsoil from being washed away during watering.

Planting Procedures

1. Cuttings should be taken from strong, healthy branches that are fully leafed. The cuttings should be snipped from the branch, as shown above, and should be about $2\frac{1}{2}''$ in length. About $\frac{3}{4}$ of each leaf should be cut off, leaving $\frac{1}{4}$. This is done to reduce the amount of evaporation from the leaves and to help water circulation.

2. Cut the ends of the cuttings at an angle, as shown, with a sharp knife. Also, cuts usually are made just below a leaf node. This makes it easier for the cuttings to absorb moisture and prevents rotting. It also stimulates the growth of new roots. Root hormone powder is used by some people to stimulate root growth but it is not essential to do so.

3. Plant the cuttings by thrusting the cut ends diagonally into the topsoil of your pot. About $\frac{2}{3}$ of the stem is pushed into the soil. Leave enough space between each cutting so that the leaves will not be touching. Also, do not bury any leaves.

4. Water the cuttings thoroughly with a sprinkling can, being careful not to let the force of the water knock them over. Watering should continue until some water comes out of the drainage hole.

GROWING CUTTINGS   69

  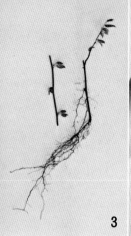 

Pot Placement and Care of Cuttings

1. After the cuttings are planted, place the pot on a flat surface protected from direct sunlight and strong wind.

2. Water the cuttings several times a day. Try to keep the leaves moist at all times. At night, the pot should be set out where it can get the night dews.

3. About two weeks after planting, the pot should be set out in the morning sunshine for a few hours every day, increasing the amount of exposure gradually.

4. After one or two months, the pot should be set outside on an ordinary flower shelf. New roots will have already started or will be about to start. The cuttings in #1 are one month old.

5. For fertilizer, a small amount of oil-meal cake is recommended after approximately six months.

Repotting

Cuttings are usually repotted when they are one year old, at which time they average almost 8″ in height. The cuttings shown in #3 allow a com-

parison between a fresh cutting and one a year old. Repotting procedures are outlined below.

1. Prepare a small pot, about $4\frac{3}{4}''$ in diameter, for each cutting by filling it $\frac{1}{4}$ full with small lumps of soil.

2. Select a cutting and pull it carefully from the large pot of cuttings, then snip off the lower part of the main root and other strong roots, as shown in #4. This is done to allow the weaker roots to become stronger, thus giving all the roots a better general balance. Do this for each cutting to be repotted.

3. Hold each year-old cutting in the center of its small pot and fill the pot with topsoil.

4. Water the cuttings thoroughly, just as you did in the initial potting. NOTE: Year-old cuttings can be replanted in the field in much the same way as described above.

Development of Cuttings

An idea of how cuttings develop over several years can be gained from #7, which shows two dogwood cuttings. The tree on the left is two years

old and the one on the right three. Note how the cuttings take on more tree-like forms as they grow. This is seen even more clearly in #8, where the cutting on the left is four and that on the right five years old. They are already beginning to look like miniature trees.

Some Cuttings for Bonsai
The different species cultivated from cuttings shown in #9 are all three years old. From right to left are a Sargent juniper, a flowering quince, a dwarf azalea, and an Ezo spruce.

Samples of Cuttings (# 10)
From right to left, upper row: Pyracantha, Japanese bush clover, *momiji* maple, rock cotoneaster, winter jasmine, Japanese cypress, needle juniper, cape gardenia, Ezo spruce.
   From right to left, lower row: Thunberg berberry, Sargent juniper, dwarf kumquat, shrubby cinquefoil, lilac, cryptomeria, flowering quince, dogwood, azalea.

Chapter 4

GRAFTING *(tsugiki)*

GRAFTING is the method most often used for preserving fine or unusual species for bonsai or for producing a larger number of a certain species of tree. A graft is called a "scion" and the tree to which it is attached is called a "stock." In most cases, the scion is of a cultivated or fine species and the stock tree is an uncultivated version of the same species. It is a basic principle that the stock tree must be of the same species as the scion. A few examples of such graftings are a five-needle pine onto a Japanese black pine, a crab apple onto a wild crab apple, and a flowering apricot onto a wild apricot.

Methods of Grafting
There are two principal methods of grafting: top grafting and side grafting. In side grafting, the scion is grafted onto the stock tree near the roots, then after the graft takes hold the tree is cut off above the graft. In top grafting, the stock tree is cut off at an appropriate height first, then split downward slightly, and the scion inserted.

Side grafting is generally used for evergreen and top grafting for deciduous trees. Some deciduous trees can be and are grafted by the side method, however. Two other methods, the *yobi-tsugi* and the *me-tsugi* (described below) are used when one wants to add a branch or twig to the trunk or branch of a bonsai tree.

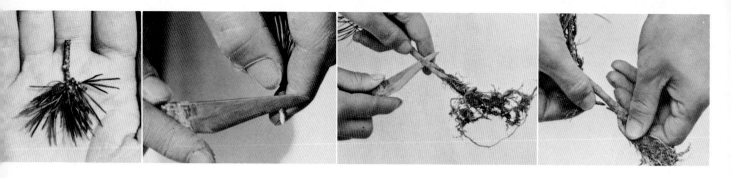

The Disadvantage of Grafts

The one major disadvantage of grafting has, in the past, been the unsightly bump formed at the joint of the scion and stock. With the development of new techniques, however, this drawback—which made grafting seem inappropriate for bonsai—has been largely overcome.

Grafting Season

Grafting for both evergreen and deciduous trees is best carried out in the spring immediately after new buds have appeared. The buds should still be firm and inactive at the time of grafting. In general, evergreen trees are grafted between the middle of February and the middle of March; other trees are usually grafted in March. Evergreens may also be grafted in early autumn, between the middle of August and the middle of September.

Side Grafting (five-needle pine onto Japanese black pine)

Let us take for our example the grafting of a Japanese white (five-needle) pine scion onto a three-year-old Japanese black pine, grown from seed, as stock. Ordinarily, a tree around 7″ in height is easy to handle as stock.

1. Make your scion by cutting off the end of a branch from a five-needle pine to a length of 2″ before the buds become active.

2. Cut the end of the scion at an angle with a sharp knife, as shown.

3. Make a slanting cut in the trunk of the stock tree near the roots (see photo).

4. Insert the scion snugly into the cut with the cut face of the scion facing the center of the stock. Resin from both the scion and the stock will bind the two together over a period of time. For this reason the insertion of the scion should be done very quickly after cutting.

5. After inserting the scion, secure the joint by wrapping it with vinyl tape.

6. Plant the stock, now with the scion attached to it, in a small pot in the same manner as described for repotting a year-old cutting. That is, first fill the pot $\frac{1}{3}$ full with lumpy soil, then hold the tree in the center of the pot and fill in around it with topsoil. Water the stock until water leaks out of the drainage hole.

Care of Side Graftings

After the stock tree is potted, keep it indoors out of the sun and wind, especially if the grafting is done in February or March, until the buds become active. Usually two months will pass before the buds on the scion start showing vitality. The vinyl tape should be left on at least one year, until the scion actually becomes part of the stock.

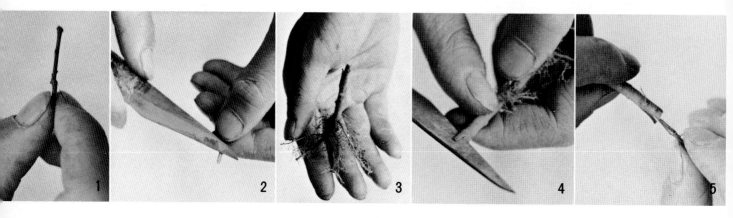

After one year has passed, if the graft has taken, the vinyl tape is removed and the stock above the graft is cut off. The remaining stock, with its scion, is cultivated and fertilized in the same manner as ordinary potted trees. This is true for all methods of grafting.

Two years from the time of grafting, the scion will start taking on the form of a bonsai.

Top Grafting (English holly onto Japanese "plum-leaf" holly)
As our example for top grafting, let us make our scion from English holly and our stock from a kind of Japanese holly called *umemodoki*.

1. Cut a scion about 2″ in length from an English holly when the buds have appeared but are still inactive.

2. Cut the end of the scion at an angle near the roots, as shown.

3. Select an *umemodoki* with a stem about the thickness of a pencil and pull it out of the ground with the roots intact. Cut the top of the tree off about 2″ above the roots.

4. Split one side of the top of the stock to an appropriate depth (see # 4).

5. Insert the scion into the split with the cut side facing the center of

6　　　7　　　8　　　9

the stock. Since the resin oozing out of the scion and the stock will bind the two together, the insertion should be done quickly.

　6. Secure the joint by wrapping it tightly with cellophane tape, then plant the stock in a pot in the same manner as described in the side-grafting method.

Care of Top Graftings

Post-potting care of top graftings is the same as that for side graftings. The scion should be almost one with the stock in a year (#8), but the tape should not be removed until the union is complete. After two years, the growth of the scion becomes quite noticeable (#9), and after three years it begins to take the shape of a bonsai (#10). Four years from the time of grafting, the joint becomes much less conspicuous (#11), and the tree takes on a more bonsai-like appearance.

Top Grafting with Thin Stock

In cases where stock of a suitable thickness is not available, thinner stock may be used by altering the technique slightly. Thin stock should be split

10

11

GRAFTING　　77

down the middle, rather than one side, to an appropriate depth. The scion, which should be about half as thick as the stock, should be cut into a wedge shape rather than at an angle. All other details are the same as described above.

Yobi-Tsugi Grafting

In the *yobi-tsugi* (inarching) method, the bark of the "parent" or stock tree and of the scion branch is cut away in the areas which are to be united. The cut areas are then tied together. There are three ways of applying this method.

1. The grafting of a long branch onto the trunk of the same tree.
2. The grafting together of two trees growing in separate pots.
3. The grafting of the branch of a natural tree onto a potted tree.

Metsugi Grafting

Metsugi or "bud" grafting is done by cutting a fan-shaped opening into the trunk or branch of a tree, then implanting a prepared bud and securing it in place. With care, the bud will grow into a branch.

1. Make a T-shaped cut with a sharp knife in the branch or trunk of an appropriate tree.
2. Prepare the bud by cutting it free from its parent, being careful to cut around it and to cut in deep enough to remove part of the inner bark of the parent.
3. Spread the T-shaped cut into a fan-shaped opening, carefully pulling the bark back on both sides.
4. Implant the prepared bud in this opening and fold the bark back into place around it.
5. Secure the bud and bark with vinyl tape.

Chapter 5

LAYERING AND DIVIDING *(toriki)*

OFTEN a natural tree, or perhaps one you are already cultivating, will have a fine branch or top that would make a wonderful bonsai if grown separately. Layering and dividing are two special methods used to develop new roots—and thus new trees—from such branches. The advantage of these techniques is that they allow a new bonsai to be grown in less time than is required for seed planting or cuttings.

These methods are also used to shorten trees with long, thin trunks without lower branches, and to alter trees in order to give them better overall balance.

Whether roots can be made to grow from the branches of trees depends on species and age. With few exceptions, however, new roots will develop on almost any tree if the layering and dividing techniques are applied with care and patience. Different techniques are used for evergreen and deciduous trees, but in either case it is mostly a matter of selecting vigorous branches and giving them time to take root.

Layering and Dividing an Evergreen (Five-needle Pine)
When layering or dividing an evergreen, a section of the trunk or branch that has a new branch or fork should be selected. These sections will take root more easily. We have selected a five-needle pine to illustrate the layering method. The purpose is to create a clump-like trunk ·system *(kabudachi)*, a type of bonsai in which a single tree appears to have several trunks growing from its roots.

1. Select a five-needle pine about five years old that has been grown from seed.

2. Wrap the section selected for layering, that is, a section where branches fork out, with copper wire. (Use #20 gauge copper wire for tree with 2 inch diameter. The thickness of wire should increase in accordance with the thickness of tree.)

3. Tighten the wire so that it bites into the tree about $\frac{1}{2}$ the thickness of the wire. This will act as a tourniquet and prevent water and sap from flowing naturally, thus forcing the section above the wire to grow new roots in its struggle for survival.

4. Prepare sufficient sphagnum moss, enough to extend out 3 times the diameter of the tree section, soak it and squeeze out the water, then wrap it around the wired section. Do not use too much moss, for it will cause the section to cool excessively and harm the tree.

5. Tie a hemp cord around the section, leaving one end long and free, securing the moss in place on top and immediately above the wire.

6. Cover the moss with a vinyl wrapper that has been perforated to allow ventilation.

7. Tie the vinyl wrapper in place with the long, free end of hemp cord,

just tight enough to hold the wrapper in place, leaving the top open for watering.

8. Only ordinary care need be given now until new roots develop, with sufficient watering from time to time to prevent the moss from drying out. Be sure the tree is exposed to ample sunshine.

Season for Layering and Dividing Evergreens
From early March to early April is the best season for layering and dividing evergreens. Although evergreens usually require more time to develop new roots than deciduous trees—six months to one year—vigorous trees will produce new roots in roughly three months.

Cutting and Planting
When a number of roots have appeared and broken through the wrapping, it is safe to cut the new tree off. Leave the moss wrapping on and cut the section off, taking special care not to injure the tender new roots.

The new tree thus created should be planted in a large pot just as if it

were a tree collected from the mountains. Leave the moss on the roots, which should not be damaged in any way, when planting.

Post-planting Care
The new tree should be kept in a partially shaded place for at least two weeks after it has been potted. After two weeks, it should be gradually exposed to more sun, preferably on an ordinary garden shelf. In a month or so, a small amount of fertilizer, such as oil-meal cake, is given to the new tree. After a year of cultivation, the moss should be removed carefully so as not to damage the roots, then the tree replanted in a pot suitable for its type and style.

Illustrated Layering and Dividing of an Ezo Spruce
   1. Ezo spruce prepared for layering and dividing.
   2. One year later, stripped of moss and repotted.
   3. Operation completed, with the tree cultivated to a height of 13″ after five years. The pot is 21½″ long.

Layering and Dividing a Deciduous Tree (white beech)

We have selected for our example a white beech that was collected in the mountains and artificially grown for some twenty years. When selecting your tree for layering and dividing, give due consideration to whether the section to be used can be trained into a regular bonsai within a year or two of the operation. The intention in our example is to produce a tree with two trunks.

1. Select that section of the trunk immediately below the forking of two branches.

2. Make two separate cuts, about 1 1/4″ apart, around the section with a knife. If the cuts are not sufficiently separated, the bark may grow back together, thus making it impossible for new roots to grow. As a rule of thumb, the distance between the two cuts should be two or three times the diameter of the trunk of the section.

3. Peel off the bark between the two cuts.

4. Neatly clean the upper cut, for the new roots will grow immediately below it.

5. Whittle the area between the two cuts to make the section thinner at the middle, cutting slightly into the heart of the trunk. Care should be taken not to cut into the trunk too deeply, or the tree may break when it is watered.

6. Tie hemp twine around the section below the whittled area, leaving the ends loose.

7. Soak a suitable amount of moss in water and squeeze most of the water from it. Wrap this moss around the cut area and cover it with vinyl, as was described for the evergreen above.

8. Spread the vinyl wrapper open at the top, then tie the wrapping and moss securely to the tree. Work upward when tying so the moss will not fall off.

9. Water the moss through the opening at the top of the wrapper.

Season for Layering and Dividing Deciduous Trees
The best season for layering and dividing deciduous trees is in the spring, either just before the new buds start to appear or after they have freshly

leafed. June, toward the end of the rainy season, is also suitable in Japan.

Ordinarily, deciduous trees will start to grow new roots from one to two months after the operation. The same care and techniques used for cutting and potting evergreens apply to deciduous trees also.

Some Pointers

In layering and dividing, whether an evergreen or deciduous tree is involved, a rough trunk should be scrubbed lightly with a stiff brush before starting. Old trees with rough or peeling bark, dead branches, or damage caused by nature should be avoided.

Chapter *6*

CARE OF BONSAI

Watering

Bonsai, because they are in pots with a limited amount of soil, require adequate watering. Carelessness in this regard is one of the main causes of withering. Not only will the lack of water and higher temperatures cause the capillary roots to wither and die, but air penetrating the dry soil will also make it more difficult for later watering to be effective, thus resulting in even more dead roots. So it is imperative that watering be adequate and timely if your bonsai is to be successful.

As a general rule, bonsai should be watered "before the surface soil becomes dry." It is commonly thought that watering is best done once a day except in the summer, when watering is done twice a day, once in the morning and once in the evening. To follow such a mechanical rule, however, is erroneous, since the condition of the soil and trees varies with the seasons and the species of tree. Watering is best done when the topsoil is still slightly damp, or more precisely, when it is about 70% dry. A lightening of color of the surface soil is a good visual indication that watering is needed. Watering should be continued until there is leakage from the drain hole.

The amount of water necessary for bonsai varies with the season. In the spring, when the trees become active and start budding, water will be required often. The condition of the soil must therefore be watched carefully. In the summer, potted soil dries out even more quickly, so water must be given in abundance frequently. Autumn watering, however, is more regular, since the trees remain in a more constant state. Because bonsai are generally kept indoors in the winter, the soil will dry quickly and require large amounts of water during that season, even though some species are dormant.

In short, the bonsai grower must be constantly alert to the condition of his soil, keeping in mind the differences of the seasons. A healthy tree will require watering periodically, and if it does not – that is, if the soil remains damp over a long period of time – it is safe to assume that there is something wrong with it. If this happens, refrain from wetting the soil too much and try to discover the cause of the problem.

Another important point in watering bonsai is the wetting of leaves. This is usually done in the summer during hot spells, when the tree is weak, or when sufficient water is not absorbed by the roots. Primarily, the method is used to make up for water lost through evaporation from the leaves, but it also washes dust from the leaves and prevents burning by the sun. By spraying water onto the tree, humidity is increased and the stomata, which close during the day, reopen, thus accelerating evaporation and lowering the temperature of the leaves. It is a good practice to spray the leaves both in the morning and in the evening, except in winter.

Feeding

Because bonsai are cultivated in limited amounts of soil, adequate feeding is necessary from time to time. As a general rule, a small amount of feed is given in the spring and a large amount in the autumn. The actual amount given, however, will depend upon the stage of cultivation of the bonsai, with larger amounts for growing bonsai and smaller amounts for mature bonsai.

Feed for bonsai should contain the three principal ingredients of nitrogen, phosphoric acid, and potash to the ratio of 50, 30, and 20, respectively. Oil-meal cake, which is often recommended for bonsai because it improves leaf color, is ideal if potash is added to it. When mixed with water and given in liquid form, nutrients must be applied frequently. The general practice, however, seems to be the heaping of the non-liquid form on the surface of the soil. Nutrients should not be applied during budding in the spring.

Manure is usually placed on the surface of the soil in small heaps, with each heap equal to about two spoonfuls. One heap is usual for each 12″ length of pot, but exact quantity is determined by the season and the age of the tree. The heaps should be placed between the tree and the edge of the pot. If the heap is too close to the tree, it may cause damage; if too close to the edge, it may be washed away during watering. When the tree is watered, the manure will be dissolved and be absorbed by the soil.

Feeding in Spring

In May and June, two heaps of oil-meal cake can be given to your bonsai as shown. A young tree is given a little more than one heap once in May and once in June. A mature tree is given a little less than one heap twice in May and twice in June. The exact amounts will depend, of course, on the size of the pot.

If the tree is of a flowering or fruit-bearing species, small additional amounts of phosphoric acid and caustic potash should be given. Fish or bone meal or a liquid fertilizer such as *Hyponex* are good for this. Fertilizer should not be given, of course, when the trees are in flower or bear fruit.

Feeding in Autumn

Feeding in autumn is done in much the same manner as in spring. Deciduous trees should be fed after the leaves have fallen but prior to the end of October. Evergreens may be fed in September and October, and sometimes as late as November. A liquid fertilizer should be applied to flowering or fruit-bearing trees, as in the spring. Fertilizing in autumn helps make bonsai trunks thicker and stronger.

Prevention of Disease and Insect Damage
As living things, bonsai are susceptible to insect attacks and disease. There are a number of preventive and corrective measures which may be taken, depending upon the type of insect, disease, and tree. A general preventive method is outlined below.

First, it is imperative to keep a bonsai in good health, since insects and bacteria tend to attack weak trees. Ample sunshine and fresh air are important. A further means of protection is to spray the tree with a general purpose fungicide that has been diluted as recommended by the makers. If the soil is dry, water the tree first, then, as with any insecticide, take care not to contaminate the soil.

When insects are found on the tree, spray with an appropriate insecticide. If the tree appears to be infected by bacteria, which is evident by sudden changes of leaf color or the appearance of sickly specks on the trunk, apply an appropriate bactericide. It is usually a good idea to thin insecticides or bactericides a little more than the instructions indicate.

Weather Protection
Protecting bonsai by keeping them indoors or partially shaded is an important part of cultivation techniques. The care of cuttings, repotted trees, and so on has been described in the respective sections, so it will suffice here to describe only protection during the winter months.

Various species, and bonsai at certain stages of cultivation, must be kept indoors during the cold season—usually December, January, and February.
These are listed below.

1. Trees whose roots are not fully grown.

2. Trees, such as pomegranate, cryptomeria, and needle juniper, which do not stand up well in cold weather.

3. Deciduous trees, such as the Zelkova and maple, which have thin, weak branches that might wither in cold weather.

4. Trees in very small pots, shallow pots, or growing on rocks.

5. Trees that will flower or bear fruit for appreciation in winter, such as the Pyracantha, whose fruit blackens in the cold.

Bonsai of the type listed above should be kept in a room with windows opening only to the south. Sunlight through glass is ideal for these trees, but it is undesirable to have the room as warm as a greenhouse. During good weather, the trees should be taken outside for fresh air and sunshine several times a week. Attention to watering is also important, since evaporation occurs rapidly indoors. Also, cold damage is caused in part by dry soil, so regular watering is necessary to maintain a correct metabolism.

Repotting
Since bonsai are grown in small pots, occasional repotting is necessary in order to provide fresh soil for the dwarf trees to develop properly. Below are listed some important reasons for repotting.

1. As a bonsai grows, it develops more and more roots which crowd the inside of the pot and sometimes start to rot. By repotting, you can loosen and reduce the number of roots.

2. The manure or fertilizer content of the soil in a bonsai pot decreases over time. This can be freshened by repotting.

3. There is also a certain loss of soil over time. By repotting, the proper amount of soil can be restored.

In short, repotting gives a bonsai tree a freshened soil environment that will improve the tree's metabolism.

Frequency of Repotting

The frequency with which a bonsai is repotted depends entirely upon its species. A few general rules are outlined below:

1. Bonsai with fast-growing roots, such as willows, or with a great water intake, such as ivy, should be repotted once a year.

2. Pine and oak trees should be repotted once every three to five years.

Season for Repotting

Repotting seasons vary with locality, but spring, when the sap starts flowing and new buds appear, is the best time. Trees coming out of their dormant state tend to survive repotting better. It is not necessary, however, to restrict yourself to spring, providing that the condition of the tree is good, the proper equipment is used, and the post-potting care is adequate. Certain species, such as the Ezo spruce and some nut varieties, may be repotted around the end of October and beginning of November. Mid-winter and mid-summer should always be avoided for repotting.

Soil for Repotting

The standard soil combinations for repotting are outlined below.

1. For pine and oak trees, a combination of 70% red loam and 30% sand-clay mixture is desirable.

2. For other species, a combination of 60% red loam, 30% black loam, and 10% well-rotted leaves is desirable.

The small lumps of soil used to line the bottom of the pot are obtained by first sieving dried red loam through a $\frac{1}{4}''$ mesh screen to remove the fine soil, then through a $\frac{3}{8}''$ mesh screen to obtain the small lumps.

Method for Repotting (Pyracantha)

For our example, we shall repot a Pyracantha. The bonsai should not be watered prior to repotting and the soil should be **dry**.

1. Loosen the soil around the inside of the pot with a thin stick. A bamboo chopstick is preferable, but any tapered stick slightly thinner than a pencil is suitable.

2. After loosening the soil in the pot, grasp the tree at the bottom of the trunk and lift it out of the pot together with the soil.

3. Place the tree on a revolving stand and carefully remove some of the soil with your stick, rotating the stand slowly. Work from the outside in, taking care not to injure the small roots.

4. Remove some of the soil from under the tree, again being careful not to injure the roots. About 70% of the soil is removed in steps 3 and 4.

5. Trim those roots that appear too vigorous, as well as those that are injured or dying.

6. Select a pot, keeping in mind the species of tree and style of bonsai. For pine, oak, or weak trees, an unglazed pot is better because it will absorb more sunlight and warm the soil inside more quickly. Cover the drainage holes with vinyl mesh and loop a piece of vinyl-covered wire through them, leaving both ends outside the pot.

7. Fill the pot about $\frac{1}{4}$ full with small lumps of soil, spreading just enough topsoil over the lumps to cover them. This layer of topsoil should be thicker if the volume of the roots is larger than pictured.

8. Place the tree, all trimmed and prepared, in the pot. If you want it to stand higher out of the pot, add more topsoil.

9. Tie the tree securely around the roots with the vinyl-covered wire to hold it in place. Try to keep the wire under the soil as much as possible.

10. Gradually add more topsoil. Use your stick to fill in soil around the roots. Tapping the side of the pot with your hand will also help.

11. When the pot is about 80% full, press the soil down lightly with your fingers.

12. Cover the topsoil with a thin layer of "decoration" soil, pressing it down around the edges of the pot with a small trowel so that none will be lost during watering.

13. Sweep the surface soil with a whisk broom so it will be flat and even.

14. Place the repotted tree in a flat, partially shaded place and water it

thoroughly. Water slowly so that the soil will absorb the moisture gradually. Water leaking from the drainage holes indicates sufficient moisture.

Care of Repotted Bonsai

Repotted bonsai should be kept in a partially shaded place for two to three weeks. New roots will have started to grow within three to six months, at which time the vinyl-covered wires should be cut off and removed. If the repotting was done in the fall, the bonsai should be moved either indoors or to a place where it can receive sufficient sunshine but be protected from the wind.

Trimming Buds and Shoots

Ideally, a bonsai should have a trunk of aged appearance and, at the same time, youthful branches and leaves. Branches are kept young and vigorous by proper repotting and adequate feeding. Proper repotting and feeding will produce not only vigorous new roots but also enliven branches and bring forth new buds. These buds must, however, be trimmed off from time to time to prevent the branches from growing and thickening, which results in unsightly branches. Occasionally, withering will also occur if buds are not adequately trimmed.

Bud Trimming for Momiji Maples and Beeches

Unlike other deciduous trees, *momiji* maples and beeches must have their buds trimmed but once a year, in the spring, unless they are quite young or fed excessively. Bud trimming should be done before the buds turn into leaves, at which time it will be too late because of the increased length between nodes.

The best time for trimming is immediately after the buds start to open and begin to curl in the process of growth. Buds are usually trimmed by pinching them off at the appropriate node with the fingernails.

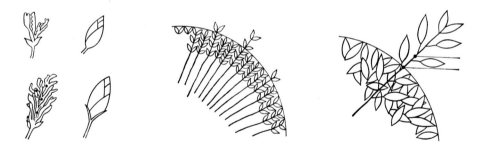

Bud Trimming for Elms, Kaede Maples, and Carpinus

Buds for elms, *kaede* maples, and carpinus should be nipped while they are still tender. Those buds growing out beyond the line formed by the branches should be nipped back until they are even with the line. Nipping should be done from time to time between April and October.

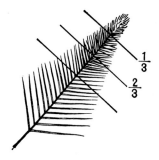

Shoot Trimming for Needle Trees
Shoots on Ezo spruce should be trimmed between the middle of April and the middle of May, and those on needle junipers and cryptomerias between spring and summer. Either $\frac{1}{3}$ or $\frac{2}{3}$ of each new shoot is trimmed off immediately after budding.

Shoot Trimming for Deciduous Trees
Buds which have been overlooked or trimmed too late may be trimmed after they have grown into shoots, in the case of deciduous trees. These shoots are trimmed off at the first or second node. Any new buds which appear on the shoots after trimming should be nipped immediately.

Shoot Trimming—Example I (Ezo spruce)

In this example, an Ezo spruce is shown just prior to shoot trimming (#1). Next, $\frac{2}{3}$ of each shoot is nipped off with the fingernails (#2), and withered, damaged, or crowded branches are pruned with scissors (#3). The branches of your bonsai should be beautifully shaped by the trimming (#4).

Trimming—Example II (carpinus)

In our second example, we have a carpinus, grown from seed, that is about six years old (#1). You can see that the branches have already grown too long. The twigs are trimmed back to either the first or second node (#2). Next, the branch growing down to the right is pruned (#3) in order to allow the branch growing out to the right to grow thicker. A tree such as this should always be trimmed. Our trimmed example is shown in #4.

CARE   99

Training Bonsai

No matter whether your bonsai are gathered from the mountains, grown from seed or cuttings, or produced by layering, training is always necessary to shape them into artistic forms. A number of training techniques— pruning, trimming, wiring, defect correction—are commonly used, as outlined below.

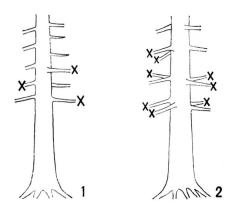

Pruning

Pruning, the traditional method of training bonsai, is used for correcting tree forms or "postures" as well as for retarding natural growth. In cases where there are two opposing branches (#1) or there are too many branches extending out at the same height in many directions (#2), pruning is required. Those branches marked with X's in the illustrations should be cut off. These examples will give you an idea of how to correct similar problems when you encounter them in training your own bonsai.

Trimming

An excess of small branches, twigs, and shoots is cured by trimming. These are usually trimmed off at the joint before they grow too large so that unsightly scars will not remain.

1. Trim young shoots growing at the forks of larger branches and the trunk (#3). Such shoots often start growing at forks in the cryptomeria and the needle juniper.

2. Trim small branches of five-needle pines. If the branches are too long, trim them back (#4). Trim overcrowded small branches and growths which are too strong from the standpoint of balance.

3. Trim small branches off Ezo spruce (#5). If the branches are too long, trim them back.

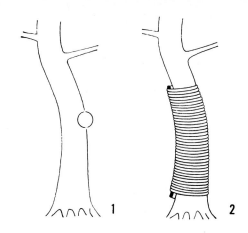
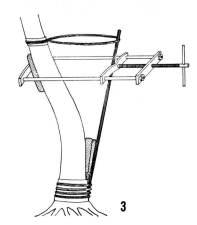

Correcting Trunk Defects

When you wish to correct a curving trunk at the spot indicated (#1), use either of the following methods.

(A) USING CORDS

You will need green hemp cord or other types of cord which will rot in two or three months and two pieces of heavy wire. Place the wires over a few strands of cord vertically on the trunk opposite of the direction in which you wish to straighten the trunk. Then wind the cord tightly around the trunk as illustrated (#2).

(B) USING A CLAMP

Besides the clamp, an iron bar, heavy cloth or pieces of old rug, a piece of zinc plate, rubber or leather to protect the trunk from being scarred, and pieces of wire are required. Wrap the base of the trunk with rubber or leather and then with a zinc plate; place the iron bar vertically on the side toward which you wish to bend the trunk and secure firmly with wire. Use heavy cloth or a thick piece of rug as padding on the trunk, put the clamp in position and gradually tighten to straighten trunk. Then wrap the trunk just above the position of the clamp with heavy cloth or a thick piece of rug, and wire the trunk to the iron bar. (#3). The clamp should be applied between October and February, when the tree is not growing, and kept on until the following June or July. By this time, any cracking of the bark caused by the straightening process will have filled in.

Wiring

Wiring, a relatively modern method of training bonsai trunks and branches into the desired forms, has become commonly accepted. It is often used in place of, or in conjunction with, the traditional methods of long-term pruning and hemp-rope binding. Wiring permits the bonsai grower to train his trees into almost any stylistic form.

Copper wire that has first been annealed in a low-temperature fire is preferred. Annealing softens the wire and helps prevent damage to tree bark. Wires of varying thicknesses are usually prepared, since the bending of trunks and branches calls for wire of appropriate size and strength. Some trees require wiring while they are still young, so it is suggested that the wire used in this case be wrapped in paper to prevent damage to the growing branches.

Wiring Cautions

1. Weak trees or trees that have just been repotted should never be wired, for they may wither and die. Again, a tree should not be repotted soon after wiring.

2. Always wind the wire in the direction the branch is to be bent in

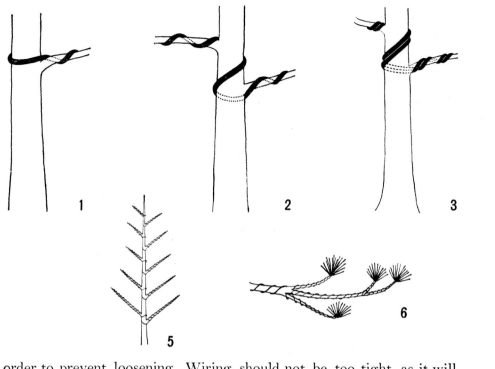

order to prevent loosening. Wiring should not be too tight, as it will injure the branch, nor too loose, as the wiring will not serve its purpose.

Figures

1. Wrapping one branch with one wire.
2. Wrapping two branches with one wire.
3. Wrapping with a second wire when one is insufficient.
4. Wrapping two wires.
5. Wrapping small branches inward toward the trunk (seen from above).
6. Straightening a shoot. Do not wire tightly.
7. Wired bonsai. Note the varying branch lengths.

1

3

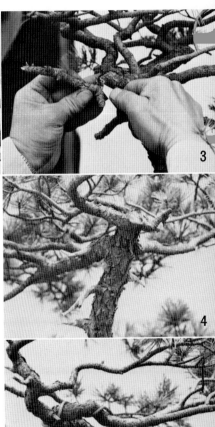

4

5

Training of Bonsai (five-needle pine)

For our example, we shall refine and style a five-needle pine which is about 50 years old, and has been transplanted and left for five years. It has the basic bonsai form but has not received any training.

1. Trim dead branches (#2).

2. Peel the bark from the ends of the trimmed branches and sharpen the exposed areas into points (##3, 4). These dead branches are called *jin*. Through contrast with the trunk, they usually give a bonsai a more interesting, elegant appearance and serve as symbols of age.

3. Before starting to wire, cut off all unnecessary branches and give your tree its basic bonsai style.

4. To bend the branch on the right down and to the right, wrap it with heavy wire down to the tip (#5).

5. Pull the branch down to the right (#6).

6. Wrap a similar wire around the branch on the left and pull it down to the left (#7).

7. To hold the branches in place, draw them toward the trunk and fasten the ends of the wire onto a small branch on the trunk (#8). When the basic wiring is completed, the tree should now look more like a regular bonsai (#9); compare it with the tree in #1.

8. If necessary, wire the smaller branches and twigs into the desired forms (#10).

9. Wrap thin wires around the twigs and straighten the shoots so that all the pine needles will face upwards (##11, 12).

10. Leave the wires in place until they start to bite into the branches—between six months and one year—then remove them and allow the tree to grow freely for about one year. After a year of free growth, the branches should be wired again. Ordinary bonsai must be wired two or three times in this manner.

Soil

The consistency, quality, and care of soil for bonsai determines the health, vitality, and appearance of your dwarf trees. Ideally, soil for bonsai should be lumpy, should drain easily, and should usually be free of manure or artificial fertilizer.

Red loam: Brownish-red soil with hard, solid lumps; free of manure. Used as the basic soil for bonsai. Screened into three grades: large, medium, and small lumps.

Sand-and-clay mixture (Kiryu-tsuchi): Resembles red loam, but grayish in color and sandy in texture with hard lumps. Usually mixed with red loam to produce soil for evergreen bonsai. Screened into three grades: large, medium, and small lumps.

Black loam: Dark brown soil with hard, solid lumps; some manure content. Mixed with red loam to produce soil for various types of bonsai and, when finer lumps are used, for decoration soil. Screened into three grades: large, medium, and small lumps.

Sandy light clay (Kanuma-tsuchi): Yellowish-white soil—turning yellowish-brown when damp—capable of retaining large amounts of moisture. When screened and mixed with 30% sphagnum or "mountain" moss, it is used for planting azaleas, and when mixed with red loam, for cultivating cuttings.

Screening

Soil for bonsai may be purchased at a nursery or garden supply shop, or it may be dug out of a suitable natural source. Prior to screening, all the soil types described above should be dried. This is usually done by spreading the soil on straw mats and exposing it to the sun and wind for about ten days. After screening, lumps that are very large or very fine should be discarded, leaving only the three grades of large, medium, and small. For large grade, a mesh of 1/2″ should be used; for medium grade, 3/8″; and for small grade, 1/4″.

It is always best to use soil of the same type found in the natural environment in which a particular species grows. Since it is often impossible to create such soil artificially, however, red loam is usually used as a substitute in bonsai cultivation. Red loam can be used either as it is or with a mixture of pumice, small pebbles or river sand to improve its drainage capacity, or of sphagnum moss to improve moisture retention.

Chapter 7
GROUP PLANTING OF BONSAI *(yose-ue)*

Bonsai do not always have to be planted as single trees. Several trees are sometimes grouped together in a flat, shallow tray to create the impression of a scenic view. This style of bonsai is called *yose-ue* or "group" planting. Commonly used trees are Ezo spruce, needle juniper, cryptomeria, Japanese gray-bark elm, maple, white beech, and carpinus.

From the standpoints of appearance and cultivation, it is considered best to limit group bonsai to one species, although evergreen and deciduous trees are sometimes planted together for an unusual and interesting effect. Such evergreens as the Ezo spruce, needle juniper, and cryptomeria are noted for their delicate leaves and their ever-changing beauty. In contrast, such deciduous trees as the Japanese gray-bark elm, maple, white beech, and carpinus offer seasonal variations, with new buds in the spring, bright green leaves in the summer, russet leaves in the autumn, and bare branches in the winter.

Season for Group Planting
The usual and best time for group planting most specimens is in spring, just before the new buds appear and have become firm.

Selection of Trees
For group planting, the best evergreens are those which have been collected from the mountains and cultivated for four or five years. Deciduous trees cultivated from seeds or cuttings are preferred for group planting.

In either case, the trees must be planted in groups before their roots have grown too extensively.

Ordinarily, the number of trees planted in groups ranges from five to fifteen, and for the sake of esthetic balance, group bonsai are usually planted in odd numbers. Although the ideal is to create the impression of a large copse or forest, for example, with only a small number of trees, the most important consideration lies in the balance between the tray and the trees.

It is a good idea to prepare a larger number of varied trees—tall and short, thick and thin, large and small—than is necessary, so that when you are ready to plant a group you will be able to select those best suited for the purpose.

Group Planting (Ezo spruce)
For our example of group planting we have selected nine Ezo spruce that

were originally collected in the mountains and cultivated for seven years. Their total age is thought to be 20 years. The trees for your group planting need not be as tall (the highest here is about 24″) or as old. If your trees are younger and shorter, you need only be careful to plant them in a suitable pot so as to give them a balanced appearance.

1. Trim off short or weak branches. This operation is necessary because the simplicity and straightness of tree trunks is an important esthetic point in group bonsai.

2. Carefully pull the trees out of their pots and tap the roots against the ground to knock off the coarser soil. Then, with a pair of chopsticks or similar tool, remove much of the soil remaining around the roots.

3. Loosen the cluster of roots by inserting your chopsticks in from underneath. Be careful to leave intact the upper roots, which have strong powers of growth. If necessary, the lower roots may even be trimmed.

GROUP PLANTING   113

4. Trim the thick main root shorter with a pair of root cutters. Do this carefully for each tree.

5. Trim the other subsidiary roots. Since the thin roots growing immediately around the bottom of the trunk have the most vitality, they should be preserved. Trim off the thicker roots beneath these with a pair of scissors. This trimming is necessary in order to fit all the trees into the group tray.

6. Prepare your tray by affixing vinyl mesh with wire over the drainage holes. Fill the tray about $\frac{1}{8}$ full with small lumps of soil.

7. Spread topsoil over the lumps in a thin layer.

8. Position the largest, best-shaped tree about $\frac{1}{3}$ the length of the pot from either the left or right end. This is the "principal" tree (1).

9. Place a shorter tree to the right and in back of the principal tree. This is called an "annex" tree (2).

10. Place another tree, smaller than the annex, to one side of both the

principal and annex. This is called a "jumper" tree (3), and together with the principal and annex it constitutes the basic composition of group planting. We are now ready to place other trees around the principal, being careful to position them at varying distances from one another so that they will have a natural appearance.

11. One short tree (4) is placed to the left and behind the principal, then another (5) to the right and front of the annex.

12. Place a short tree (6) to the right and front of the jumper so that it is not in a direct line from the principal. Be careful, also, to place it at a distance different from that between the annex and the tree (5) placed to the right and front of it.

13. Place a small, thin tree (7) to the right and behind the jumper, then another (8) to the left and behind the annex.

14. Finally, place the shortest and thinnest tree (9) close to the right corner of the tray. Because so many trees must be planted in a pattern in one

small area, care should be taken not to let the roots bunch up in the middle of the tray. Try to lead the roots toward the center and the edge of the tray, and to the right and left of one another.

15. Start filling the tray with topsoil and fix the positions of the trees. If you think some might move, secure them temporarily with wire.

16. Use a pair of chopsticks or a tool to push the soil down around the roots. An effort should be made to firmly balance the roots, while at the same time to keep the branches from intertwining. Above all, the trunks should be made to stand straight.

17. When the group of trees has been planted, water them with a sprinkling can just enough to dampen the surface soil.

18. Remove some of the surface soil from around the thicker roots so that they will appear to be strongly supporting the trees.

19. Fill in the space around the roots with peat. A little peat is also

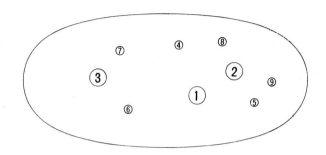

pasted to the shorter exposed roots. This is done both to accentuate the appearance and to make the peat work as a binding agent for the moss which is added next. Without the peat, the moss will slip off when the tree is watered.

20. Soak a large handful of sphagnum moss and squeeze the water out of it. This moss is patted onto the surface of the soil and over the roots to help the soil retain moisture and to give the tray a more interesting appearance. Use a small trowel to level out the soil along the edge of the pot and the edges where moss has been placed. Water the tray thoroughly after the moss is in place.

Care of Group Bonsai

As in the case of ordinary repotting, newly potted group bonsai are kept partially shaded and out of reach of strong breezes for some time, then placed on a shelf. After the roots have grown and firmly taken hold—between six and twelve months—train the trees by using the wiring method. Unnecessary or undesirable branches are trimmed to prevent intertwining. If the group was planted in the spring, training should start in the autumn, and vice versa.

Chapter 8

ROCK-GROWN BONSAI *(ishitsuki)*

Rock-grown bonsai, like all types of bonsai, are imitative reproductions of trees within a natural setting. In this case, the bonsai grow on top of rocks or in composition with rocks, usually with moss, flowers, or weeds added for effect.

A bonsai growing on top of rocks, sometimes called the "clinging-to-a-rock" type, is cultivated in soil that has been affixed to a large rock (p. 52). A basin usually containing water or sand is often used in place of a pot or tray in this case. A second variety is cultivated in soil, but arranged in a natural composition with rocks (p. 52). Both versions of the rock-grown bonsai lend themselves to such charming scenic reproductions as valleys, mountains, seashores, and rocky islands. One of the more popular trees for this type in Japan is the Ezo spruce, which thrives in the northern part of the country, despite adverse weather conditions, and manifests a wonderful vitality.

Season for Rock-grown Bonsai
Spring, just before budding, is the best season for creating rock-grown bonsai.

Selecting Trees and Rocks
Almost any species of tree may be used for rock-grown bonsai, but ideally your tree should be selected for its suitability in re-creating such natural scenes in miniature as valleys, cliffs, islands, and so forth. Another consideration in your selection should be the presence of abundant branches

and foliage. Leafy trees with many branches are more suitable for creating the impression of grand scenery—despite the smallness of the materials used. Rough, large-leafed trees with sparse branches are not suitable.

Young trees, small in size, that have been grown from seed or cuttings for some five or six years are more easily adapted to the rock-and-tree theme. Older trees, however, may also be made into fine "clinging-to-a-rock" bonsai.

In selecting a suitable rock, volcanic rocks or salt-saturated rocks from the seashore should be avoided. Good rocks for use with bonsai are usually found in the mountains, valleys, and dry river beds. Rough-textured rocks with irregular surfaces are the most suitable, since soil adheres more easily to them. They are also more interesting in appearance.

The soil affixed to rocks is actually a combination of black peat and red loam, mixed in a 50–50 ratio. When properly prepared, this soil should stick to your rock with little difficulty.

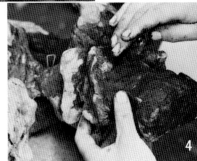

Creating a Rock-grown Bonsai (Ezo spruce)

For our example, we have selected an Ezo spruce and a large rock of unusual shape (#1). The rock is about 16″ long and 7″ high. A revolving stand, or an empty wooden box, should be prepared as a work table. Other necessary materials are copper and vinyl-covered wire and a few pieces of lead.

1. Prepare your soil by mixing well equal amounts of black peat and red loam. (#2)

2. Place your rock on the work table and fasten a suitable number of copper-wire loops to the rock with pieces of lead. This is done by holding the loops in place, then driving the lead into the rock cavities in such a way as to secure the loops (#3). These copper "root-fasteners" serve as anchors for the vinyl-covered wires that will be used to hold the roots in place. Be careful to position them at angles so they will hold down the roots properly.

3. Soak the rock in water, after all the root-fasteners are in place, then

affix your soil mixture to those parts of the rock where the roots will grow (#4)

4. Pass vinyl-covered wires through the root-fasteners, as shown (#5), and secure them by twisting. The ends should be left loose (#6).

5. Prepare your tree (this one was grown from a cutting), but do not trim the roots (#7).

6. Position the tree in a suitable place on the rock, pressing the longer roots around the rock. If there is not enough room, the roots may be folded back and overlapped.

7. Apply more soil on top of the roots (#8).

8. Secure the roots firmly in place with the vinyl-covered wires, cutting off any long ends, and cover them with soil (##9, 10).

9. A little color may be added by arranging a few *Kirishima* azaleas or wild grasses on the rock (#11).

10. When the basic arrangement is finished, freely apply soil to provide

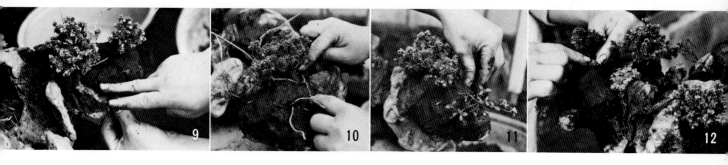

a good foundation for cultivation. The roots should be completely covered.

11. Wet moss is now laid over the soil, starting near the bottom of the trunk (#12). The soil should be covered completely in order to prevent drying and to provide a more interesting appearance. Moss applied to slanted or vertical surfaces may be held in place by V-shaped handmade pins.

12. Place the completed "clinging-to-a-rock" bonsai in a basin of water —or leave it as it is, if you prefer—for appreciation.

ROCK-GROWN   123

Care of Rock-grown Bonsai

Newly created "clinging-to-a-rock" bonsai should be kept in a partially shady place out of the wind for at least two weeks. It is during this period that the moss will regain its vigor and the roots will take hold.

Ordinarily, when a tree is repotted the weaker roots are trimmed off, which helps the tree in its struggle to grow by leaving only vigorous roots. With rock-grown bonsai, however, all roots are retained, thus creating a situation in which they can be easily injured. Consequently, this type of bonsai is weaker than others and requires more attention, especially in regard to watering. Because the roots function less efficiently in absorbing water, the moss must not be allowed to dry out. Excessive watering, at the same time, can also be harmful, since it tends to cool the roots too much. Care should be taken to water the plants gently so as not to wash away the moss or soil.

The best method for watering this type of bonsai is to spray the branches and leaves from above, which will help compensate for insufficient water absorption from the roots. Consider the tree properly watered if the moss is kept continually damp.

After two weeks of careful attention in a sheltered spot, the bonsai may be put out on a shelf in the sun.

Chapter 9

TOOLS AND EQUIPMENT

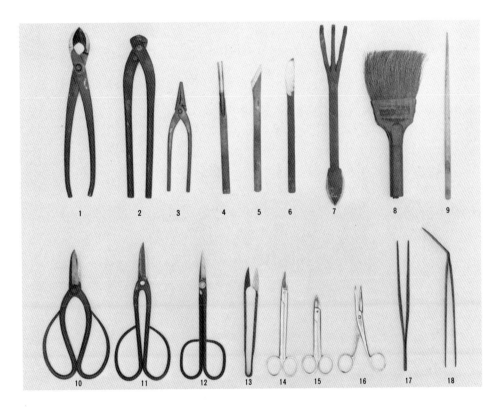

(1) Pincers for cutting heavy branches, etc.
(2) Pincers for cutting heavy wire, etc.
(3) Pliers for removing training wire from branches, etc.
(4) (5) (6) Chisels for cutting, grafting, or paring branches flush with the trunk, etc.
(7) Trowel for loosening roots.
(8) Coconut-fiber whisk for smoothing soil, etc.
(9) Bamboo chopsticks used in repotting.
(10) Snippers for cutting small branches (up to the thickness of the thumb).
(11) Long-handled snippers for trimming branches or shoots that are hard to reach.
(12) Bud-trimming snippers.
(13) Scissors for trimming leaves of all deciduous trees except flowering or fruit-bearing species.
(14) Small scissors for trimming buds.
(15) Cutter for thin wire.
(16) Scissor-shaped pliers for removing thin wire.
(17) Pincettes for removing dead leaves or weeds.
(18) Trowel-pincettes for removing dead leaves and weeds and for pressing down soil around the edge of the pot.

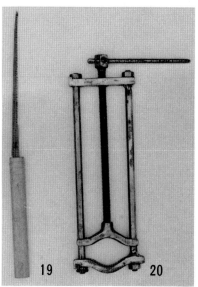
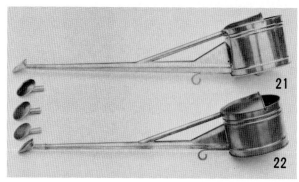

(19) Small saw for cutting thick
   branches and roots.
(20) Clamp for training thick
   trunks.
(21) (22) Watering cans.
(23) Miniature sprayer for applying disinfectants, etc.
(24) Wire.

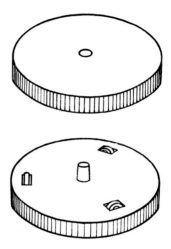

Hollow out a section in the center just large enough to fit over the peg. It should be deep enough to allow the top to ride on the casters.

A peg is fitted into the bottom part, in the center, and casters are placed around it.

Revolving stand:

A revolving stand is convenient as a worktable, since it allows one to work on a bonsai from various angles by simply turning the stand. Such a stand can be purchased, but it is also simple to make one yourself if you have two pieces of hardwood and three or four casters at hand. Oak, walnut, or any similar wood are good for this purpose.

(1) "Rice-bowl" pot
(2) Small "rice-bowl" pot
(3) Shallow round pot
(4) "Bowl" pot
(5) Shallow oval pot
(6) Small shallow oval pot
(7) Oval pot with angular interior
(8) Shallow oval pot with angular interior

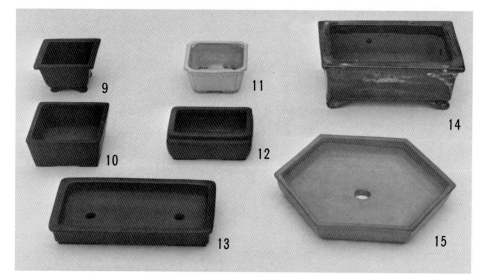

(9) Footed square pot
(10) Square pot
(11) Square pot with slit corners
(12) Rectangular pot with rounded sides
(13) Large rectangular pot
(14) Footed rectangular pot
(15) Hexagonal pot

(16) Pot shelf

APPENDICES

SPECIES	DESCRIPTION	REPOTTING	SOIL
Five-needle pine	Symbolic of Japanese scenery. Value for its refined appearance and perennial greenness.	Once every five or six years, late Mar. or autumn.	Fine red loam 60%; sand 40%
Needle Juniper	Hard trunk, leaves. Masculine appearance.	Once every two or three years, early Apr. or rainy season.	Red loam 60%; sand 40%
Black pine	Masculine appearance.	Once every four or five years in Mar., Apr. or autumn.	Fine red loam 60%; sand 40%
Red pine	Feminine and elegant appearance.	Once every four or five years in late Mar. or early Apr.	Fine red loam 60%; sand 40%
Ezo spruce	Rust-colored bark, fine needles.	Once every four to six years, early Mar., Apr., Oct., or Nov.	Fine red loam 70%; sand 30%
Sargent juniper	Grows in high mountains. Trunk bent by natural forces.	Once every two or three years, Nov. or very early spring.	Fine red loam 50%; sand 20%; limestone sand 30%
Cryptomeria	Grows straight. Noble appearance. Symbolic of mountains.	Once every two to four years in Apr. Avoid autumn and spring.	Fine red loam 70%; sand 20% leaf mould 10%
Japanese cypress	Beautiful patterns on leaves.	Once every three years, late Mar.	Fine red loam 80%; sand 20%
Japanese yew	Contrast between old, refined-looking bark and leafy foliage.	Once every other year, late Mar.	Fine red loam 70%; sand 30%, or loam 60%; sand 40%
Hemlock spruce	Member of pine family. Old yet light, cheerful appearance.	Young tree repotted once every other year, old tree once every three or four years, late Mar.–May.	Red loam 60%; sand 40% Fine red loam 60%; sand 40%

BONSAI

FEEDING	BUD TRIMMING	TRAINING	INSECT/DISEASE	REMARKS
Two or three times in spring; once in autumn.	Nip overgrown buds before they open.	Oct.–Apr.	Spider mites Needle cast	Pick off buds thoroughly in June if tree is strong and healthy.
Dry fertilizer in spring and autumn.	Nip overgrown buds occasionally.	Any time when warm.	Spider mites	Protect from wintry winds and dry air.
Two or three times in spring, once in autumn.	Nip buds before they open.	Winter	Scale insects Witches'-broom	
Apr. and May. Once in Sept. Avoid rainy season and summer.	Nip buds before they open.	Oct.; following Apr.	Spider mites, scale insects Needle cast	
Continuous feeding Apr.–Nov., except rainy season.	Trim in July to leave flower buds.	Oct.; following Apr.	Spider mites Witches'-broom	
Mar.–May. Also in autumn.	Pluck overgrown buds while soft.	Winter	Spider mites	
Apr. to Oct.	Nip overgrown buds occasionally.	Avoid autumn and winter.	Spider mites Blight	
Apr. and in autumn.	Trim twigs with too many leaves at end.	Late March.	Pestalotia disease	
Apr.–May. Also liquid feeding twice in autumn.	Trim unhealthy long branches occasionally.	Oct. and May.	Relatively free of insects	
Thinned liquid fertilizer when buds come out. Feeding in June and Oct.	Shoots grow fast. Trim long shoots to about $\frac{3}{4}''$.	Trim branches and wire in Oct.	Relatively free of insects	

SPECIES	DESCRIPTION	REPOTTING	SOIL
Kaede maple	Beauty of leaves; especially young or reddened leaves.	Once every two or three years, late Mar.	Loam or red soil 60–70%; sand 30–40%
Momiji maple	Beauty of leaves, like *kaede* maple. Red leaves considered "king of leaves."	Once every year or every other.	Red soil 80%; sand 20%
Wax tree	Beautiful reddening of leaves in autumn.	Yearly for those in small or shallow pots; once every other year for those in large pots, late Mar.	Sand 20%; any soil 80%
Maiden hair	Seasonally, bare: green leaves, and yellow leaves.	Yearly, in late Mar.	Fine red loam 60%; loam 30%; sand 10%
Ivy	Glossy green leaves.	Yearly, before budding.	Red soil 60%; sand 20%; leaf mould 20%
Zelkova tree	Tall tree with fan-shaped branches. Bare in winter.	Once every other year, late Mar.	Loam or red 70%; sand 30%
Beech	Brownish, dead leaves on the tree have their own beauty.	Once every or every other year before budding.	Red soil 70%; sand 30%
Carpinus	Most beautiful when buds come out in spring. Light red and yellow leaves in autumn. Best suited for group planting.	Once every other year, mid-Mar.	Red soil or loam 80%; sand 20%

BONSAI

FEEDING	BUD TRIMMING	TRAINING	INSECT/DISEASE	REMARKS
Excessive fertilizer Apr. and Oct. causes branches to be either too strong or too weak.	Occasionally nip overgrown buds.	Best during rainy season.	Scale insects, white-spotted longicorn	
Sufficient fertilizer in Oct. Excessive fertilizer causes thick branches.	Occasionally.	During rainy season when tree is soft.	Scale insects, white-spotted longicorn	
Modicum of fertilizer occasionally.	Nip buds and prune long branches occasionally.	Wiring any time.	Relatively free of insects	
Ocasionally, with constant manuring.	Cut off unhealthy long branches. Leave short flowering branches.	Branches in Mar. Wiring new twigs in early summer.	Pestalotia disease violet root rot	Cutting to be planted late Mar.
Spring and autumn.	Occasionally.	Trim growing vines.	Boston ivy tiger-moth	Cuttings should be cut in mid-winter and kept in water until late Mar., when they are planted.
Excessive feeding causes gnarls at joints. Insufficient fertilizer causes irregular branch tips.	Cut long vines.	Any time.	Aphids	Wire loosely. Must be taken off as soon as possible.
A modicum, occasionally.	Cut off tips of overgrown buds early.	Scissor pruning.	Relatively free of insects	
Dry and liquid fertilizer in Apr. and Sept. Avoid excessive feeding.	Nip buds before they open.	Winter to rainy season.	Aphids	Occasionally shorten unhealthy long branches.

SPECIES	DESCRIPTION	REPOTTING	SOIL
Plum	Red or white blossoms before spring. Interesting branches.	Once every year or every other year immediately after blossoms fall.	Fine red loam 50%; loam 20%; sand 20%; leaf mould 10%
Winter jasmine	Sharp, yellow 6-petal blossoms in early spring before any leaves. Stems somewhat resemble ivy.	Yearly, before or after blossoms, or in late Sept.	Fine red loam 50%; sand 30%; leaf mould 20%
Cherry	Symbol of Japan. Beautiful blossoms every spring.	Yearly, in Oct. or before budding.	Loam 40%; fine red loam 20%; sand 20%; leaf mould 20%
Flowering quince	Scarlet or thin red florets on simple, stout branches in winter or spring.	Yearly, in Oct.	Red loam 50%; sand 50%
Satsuki azalea	Member of azalea family. Elementary for bonsai. Blossoms between mid-May and mid-June.	Once every year or every other year in early spring or after blossoms.	Kanuma soil mixed with moss
Crab apple	Thin red pipe-shaped blossoms Apr.–May.	Yearly, late Mar.	Loam 50%; red loam 50%
Dwarf rhododendron	Deciduous bush in high mountains. White or thin red blossoms in center of oblong smooth leaves in early summer.	Every other year in early Apr.	Fine red loam 50%; (volcanic) sand 50%
Crape myrtle	Smooth bark. Scarlet-purple florets July–Sept.	Yearly, in late Apr.	Loam 40%; red loam 40%; sand 20%
Camellia	Lovely scarlet or white flowers in winter or spring.	Yearly, Apr. and autumn.	Fine red loam 60%; sand 20%; leaf mould 20%

BONSAI—DECIDUOUS

FEEDING	BUD TRIMMING	TRAINING	INSECT/DISEASE	REMARKS
Twice after three weeks repotting till May. Liquid Sept. and Oct.	Trim after flowering. Do not nip buds, trim with flowers in mind.	Winter. New twigs in Sept.	*Ume* cankerworm, *ume* bud moth	
Dry fertilizer in spring; sufficient liquid fertilizer in Oct. Avoid rainy season.	Occasionally trim sickly overgrown branches. Prune old branches after blossoms fall.	After blossoms, at same time as branch trimming.	Longicorn beetles	
Twice between budding and rainy season. Twice in autumn.	After blossoms. Leave a little of blossoming branches; cut the rest.	In winter after blossoms.	Black-marked prominent	Wrap paper-covered wire loosely for wiring operation.
Dry fertilizer occasionally, except in rainy season.	Nip overgrown buds only.	Scissor pruning.	Mulberry bagworm Rust	
Liquid for flower in spring. Dry fertilizer occasionally, except rainy season.	After blossoms fall.	Only in spring and summer.	Azalea lace bug, rose arge, spider mites	Buds in early July. Branches of old trees break easily, so handle with care.
Dry or liquid fertilizer from spring to rainy season. Liquid fertilizer in Sept.	Match branch ends after blossoms fall. Shorten long branches after June.	Old branches in winter. New twigs in June.	Aphids	
Two or three times in spring. Dry fertilizer in autumn.	Shorten flowering branches after blossoming.	Scissor-prune branches unfit for wiring.	Azalea cottony scale	In summer, place in cool place. Sufficient water with good drainage.
Amount depends on bud conditions. Sufficient in autumn.	After blossoms fall.	In summer, after flowers fall.	Crape myrtle scale, oriental moth, aphids	Shorter old branches on vigorous tree for more flowers.
Liquid fertilizer occasionally, spring and autumn.	Trim in July to leave flower buds.	During rainy season.	Oriental moth, tea tussock moth	Plant cuttings when buds become firm.

SPECIES	DESCRIPTION	REPOTTING	SOIL	FEEDING
Boxthorn	Numerous red fruit in summer.	Late March.	Any type with sand 30%. Pot with good drainage	Keep feeding constantly. Add extra super-phosphate.
Elaeagnus	Numerous small red fruit in summer.	Late March.	Loam 60%; sand 40%	Occasionally, as much as deemed necessary.
Dwarf kumquat Ardisia	Dwarf kumquat, bearing oblong orange-colored fruit in late autumn.	In Apr. after weather becomes warm enough.	Loam and leaf mould with a little sand	Continuous dry and liquid fertilizer except when bearing fruit. Abundant phosphorous.
Chinese quince	Red buds and white flowers. Large fruit autumn–winter.	Yearly, in spring, late Sept. or Oct.	Loam 60%; sand 20%; leaf mould 20%	Modicum after repotting. No fertilizer after flowers. Phosphate after bearing fruit.
Pomegranate	Deep scarlet flowers in summer. Fist-size fruit in autumn which burst open when ripe.	In Apr., warm weather.	Fine red loam 70%; sand 30%	Occasionally. Abundant phosphate.
Jujube	Thin yellow florets in June or July. Green oblong fruit ripen in autumn.	Yearly, in early Apr.	Loam 30%; red soil 30%; leaf mould 20%; sand 20%	Fish meal after repotting. Feed once a month after fruit ripen.
Pear	White, neat blossoms in early summer. Large fruit summer and autumn.	Yearly, immediately before buds come out.	Loam 30%; red soil 30%; leaf mould 20%; sand 20%	Fish meal after repotting. Feed once a month after fruit ripen.
Japanese spindle	Deep scarlet fruit in autumn.	Yearly, before budding.	Loam and red soil with sand 20%	Occasionally. Add fish meal to produce more and better fruit.
False bittersweet	Numerous small red fruit in autumn.	Once every year or every other year in late March.	Fine red loam 70%; sand 30%	Dry fertilizer occasionally.

BONSAI—DECIDUOUS

BUD TRIMMING	TRAINING	INSECT/DISEASE	REMARKS
To produce more fruit on new branches, shorten old branches when repotted in summer.	Avoid damaging old branches, as they break easily.	Scale insects	Summer repotting produces good results.
Cut off long branches after flowering and when tree starts to bear fruit.	Occasionally.	Scale insects	
Cut off unhealthy long branches as they never bear fruit. Leave only thick, short leaves.	Summer.	Arrowhead scale, margaroded scale, smaller citrus dog, citrus dog, yellow-patched swallowtail, citrus leaf miner.	Must be protected against cold weather.
Preserve only short, flowering branches.	Branches should not be bent.	Aphids.	
Shorten sickly long branches after flowers bloom.	Summer.	Thick-legged moth, oriental leopard moth, scale insects.	Shorten unnecessary branches to produce more fruit.
Cut extra branches after flowering buds appear.	Scissor pruning in winter.	Relatively free of insects and diseases.	
Shorten sickly long branches, leave short, flowering branches.	Scissor pruning in winter.	Scale insects, aphids. Rust.	Prone to disease and insects. Lime-sulphur mixture in spring; disinfect and spray occasionally.
Shorten non-flowering branches.	No wiring.	Scale insects.	
Shorten long vines.	Only scissor pruning.	Pellucid zygaenid, tea tortrix.	

Pests and Insects

aphids	*Aphididae*	spider mites	*Tetranychidae*
arrowhead scale	*Unaspis yanonensis*	tea tortrix	*Homoma*
azalea cottony scale	*Phenacoccus azaleae*		*magnanima*
		tea tussock moth	*Euproctis*
azalea lace bug	*Stephanitis pyrioides*		*pseudoconspersa*
		thick-legged moth	*Parallelia stuposa*
black-marked prominent	*Phalera flavescens*	*ume* bud moth	*Illiberis nigra*
		ume cankerworm	*Cystidia couaggaria eurimede*
blue leaf beetle	*Linaeidea aenea*		
Boston ivy tiger-moth	*Seudyra subflava*	white-spotted longicorn	*Anoplophora malasiaca*
citrus dog	*Papilio protenor*	yellow-patched swallowtail	*Papilio helenus*
citrus leaf miner	*Phyllocnistis citrella*		
crape myrtle scale	*Eriococcus lagerstroemiae*		

Common Diseases

longicorn beetles	*Cerambycidae*	blight	*Cercospora cryptomeriae*
margaroded scale	*Icerya purchasi*	needle cast	*Lophodermium pinastri*
mulberry bagworm	*Canephora asiatica*		
oriental leopard moth	*Zeuzera leuconotum*	Pestalotia disease	*Pestalotia chamaecyparidis*
oriental moth	*Cnidocampa flavescens*	Pestalotia disease	*Pestalotia ginkgo*
pellucid zygaenid	*Pryeria sinica*	rust	*Gymnosporangium haraeanum*
red wax scale	*Ceroplastes rubens*		
rose arge	*Arge pagana*	violet root rot	*Helicobasidium mompa*
scale insects	*Coccidea*		
scale insects	*Lepidosapinae*	witches'-broom	*Melampsorella caryophyllacearum*
smaller citrus dog	*Papilio xuthus*		

Tokyo Weather Chart

	AVERAGE TEMPERATURE		HUMIDITY	AMOUNT OF RAIN
January	37.4 F	(3.0) C	62	48 mm
February	38.7	(3.7)	62	74
March	44.6	(7.0)	66	107
April	54.7	(12.6)	72	135
May	62.2	(16.8)	76	148
June	69.1	(20.6)	80	166
July	75.9	(24.4)	82	141
August	78.4	(25.8)	81	152
September	71.8	(22.1)	82	233
October	61.2	(16.2)	79	208
November	51.3	(10.7)	74	97
December	41.7	(5.4)	67	55

NOTE: *European readers should relate the months given in the text for carrying out cultural operations to the temperatures in the above chart and make the necessary adjustments to their own conditions and locations.*

Plant Names

Ardisia	*tachibana*	*Ardisia crispa* DC.
Azaleas	*iso-tsutsuji*	*Ledum palustre* L. *var. nipponicum* Nakai
	kome-tsutsuji	*Rhododendron Tschonoskii* Maxim.
	renge-tsutsuji	*Rhododendron japonicum* Suringer
	unzen-tsutsuji	*Rhododendron serpyllifolium* Miq.
	yama-tsutsuji	*Rhododendron Kaempferi* Planch.
Azalea, dwarf	*miyama-kirishima*	*Rhododendron kiusianum* Makino
Azalea, *satsuki*	*satsuki*	*Rhododendron indicum* Sweet
Beech	*buna*	*Fagus crenata* Blume
Berberry, Thunberg	*shōbyaku* or *megi*	*Berberis Thunbergii* DC.
Bittersweet, false	*tsuru-umemodoki*	*Celastrus orbiculatus* Thunb.
Boxthorn	*kuko*	*Lycium chinense* Mill
Bush clover, Japanese	*hagi*	*Lespedeza bicolor* Turcz. *var. japonica* Nakai
Caltha	*enkōsō*	*Caltha sibirica* Makino *var. membranacea* Makino
Camellia	*tsubaki*	*Camellia japonica* L.
Carpinus	*soro*	*Carpinus laxiflora* Blume
Carpinus, Japanese	*kumashide* or *kanashide*	*Carpinus japonica* Blume
Cherry	*sakura*	*Prunus donarium* Sieb. *var. spontanea* Makino
Cinquefoil, shrubby	*kinrobai*	*Potentilla fruticosa* Rydb.
Cotoneaster, rock	*beni-shitan*	*Cotoneaster horizontalis* Decn.
Crab apple	*kaidō*	*Malus spontanea* Makino
Cryptomeria	*sugi*	*Cryptomeria japonica* D. Don
Cypress, Japanese	*hinoki*	*Chamaecyparis obtusa* Endl.
Dogwood	*mizuki*	*Cornus controversa* Hemsl.
Elaeagnus	*gumi*	*Elaeagnus pungens* Thunb.

Gardenia, cape	*kuchinashi*	*Gardenia jasminoides* Ellis *f. grandiflora* Makino
Holly	*umemodoki*	*Ilex serrata* Thunb. *var. Sieboldii* Loesn.
Ivy	*tsuta*	*Parthenocissus tricuspidata* Planch.
Jasmine, winter	*ōbai*	*Jasminum nudiflorum* Lindl.
Judas tree, Japanese	*katsura*	*Cercidiphyllum japonicum* Sieb. et Zucc.
Juniper, needle	*toshō*	*Juniperus rigida* Sieb. et Zucc.
Juniper, Sargent	*shinpaku*	*Juniperus chinensis* L. *var. Sargenti* Henry
Jujube	*natsume*	*Zizyphus Jujuba* Mill. *var. inermis* Rehd.
Kumquat	*kinkan*	*Fortunella japonica* Swingle *var. margarita* Makino
Kumquat, dwarf	*kinyuzu*	*Citrus Junos* Tanaka
Lilac	lilac	*Syringa vulgaris* L.
Maiden hair	*ichō*	*Ginkgo biloba* L.
Maple, *kaede*	*kaede*	*Acer Buergerianum* Miq.
Maple, *momiji*	*momiji*	*Acer palmatum* Thunb. *var. Matsumurae* Makino
Mulberry	*himekuwa*	*Morus bombycis* Koidz.
Myrtle, crape	*hyakujikkō*	*Lagerstroemia indica* L.
Pear	*nashi*	*Pyrus serotina* Rehder
Pine, black	*kuro-matsu*	*Pinus Thunbergii* Parl.
Pine, five-needle	*goyō-matsu*	*Pinus pentaphylla* Mayr. *var. Himekomatsu* Makino
Pine, *nishiki* black	*nishiki-matsu*	*Pinus Thunbergii* Parl. *var. corticosa* Makino
Pine, red	*aka-matsu*	*Pinus densiflora* Sieb. et Zucc.
Plum	*ume*	*Prunus Mume* Sieb. et Zucc.
Pomegranate	*zakuro*	*Punica Granatum* L.
Pourthiaea	*kamatsuka*	*Pourthiaea villosa* Decne.
Pyracantha	*tachibana-modoki*	*Pyracantha angustifolia* Schneid.
Quince, Chinese	*karin*	*Pseudocydonia sinensis* Schneid.
Quince, flowering	*boke*	*Chaenomeles lagenaria* Koidz.
Quince, Japanese	*chōjubai*	*Chaenomeles speciosa* Nakai Lindl.
Rhododendron, dwarf	*shakunage*	*Rhododendron Metternichi* Sieb. et Zucc.
Spindle, Japanese	*mayumi*	*Euonymus Sieboldiana* Blume
Spruce, *Ezo*	*ezo-matsu*	*Picea jezoensis* Carr.

Spruce, hemlock	*tsuge*	*Buxus microphylla* Sieb. et Zucc. *var. suffruticosa* Makino
Wax tree	*haze*	*Rhus succedanea* L.
Willow	*yanagi*	*Salix babylonica* L.
Yew, Japanese	*ichii*	*Taxus cuspidata* Sieb. et Zucc.
Zelkova tree	*keyaki*	*Zelkova serrata* Makino